DEVELOPING YOUR EMOTIONAL INTELLIGENCE

Boost your professional performance
by understanding emotions

Written by Maïlys Charlier
Translated by Carly Probert

Coaching 50MINUTES.com

50MINUTES.com

PROPEL
YOUR BUSINESS FORWARD!

NETWORKING

Effective CV Writing

Resolving Office Conflict

Boost Your Concentration

Find Your Work-Life Balance

www.50minutes.com

EMOTIONAL INTELLIGENCE

- **Problem:** How can I manage my emotions to maximise my potential and my chances for success?
- **Uses:** High emotional intelligence is a more certain path towards success than a large intellectual capacity.
- **Professional context:** Teamwork, team management, interviews.
- **FAQs:**
- What impact does stress have on my emotions and how can I handle it?
- Why is empathy an essential element of the development of my emotional quotient?
- What skills will enable me to grow within my company?
- How can I put a strong emotion, such as anger, to good use?
- How can I give constructive criticism to a co-worker?
- How can I use my emotions as a source of self-motivation?

> "In my previous job, I did not feel respected and I let the situation fester. I did not say anything until my supervisor pushed me too far one day while I was working a stand at an event and I exploded. I was unpleasant and I yelled at my superior in front of customers. She had pushed me so far over the edge for weeks leading up to that time, so I was unable to restrain myself and told her exactly what I thought. Two days later, I received my P45." – Rachel, administrative assistant for a non-profit organisation

In 1996, the concept of "emotional intelligence" (EI) was popularised by the book of the same name by the

American psychologist Daniel Goleman (born in 1946). He distinguishes between two kinds of intelligence: rational and emotional, measured by intelligence quotient (IQ) and emotional quotient (EQ) respectively.

According to Goleman, emotional intelligence is "the ability [...] to identify, access and control one's own emotions and those of others in a group". Therefore, emotional quotient measures the ability of an individual to use their personal skills (empathy, confidence, motivation, etc.) and social skills (communication, interpersonal relationships, etc.).

To the American psychologist, emotional quotient and intelligence quotient are not incompatible: they are simply two different ways of measuring the overall intelligence of an individual. As with a person's IQ, his theory assumes that we are born with a certain emotional quotient, with some emotional qualities and propensities inscribed in our genetic makeup. We are therefore not all equal in emotional intelligence. However, although it is very difficult to increase your IQ, there are several methods that you can use to increase your EQ. These methods not only help you to become aware of your own emotions and control them, but also to read those of others and act accordingly. Becoming emotionally intelligent is therefore within everyone's reach.

Today, many people consider EQ to be just as important as IQ, particularly in the workplace. Indeed, Goleman adds that emotional intelligence means being able to "manage feelings in order to express them appropriately and effectively, to allow others to collaborate harmoniously with common goals". Therefore, the better we are at managing our emotions (stress, sadness, anger, fear, etc.), the better we will interact with others. A team leader capable of great empathy will likely be able to reduce the stress of their employees, whilst filling them with energy: making good use of their emotions, they maximise their potential as a leader. Similarly, someone with a high emotional quotient will find it easier to work in teams. Goleman also states that "emotional intelligence is not an addition to intellect, but multiplies it: it is the invisible, but decisive, factor in exceptional performance".

So, how can you control your emotions to maximise your potential and your chances for success? And how can emotional quotient be measured?

EMOTIONAL INTELLIGENCE: THE BASICS

WHAT IS EMOTIONAL INTELLIGENCE?

Origin and definitions

In 1983, Howard Gardner proposed his theory of multiple intelligences. Among these, he distinguished one form of intelligence "related to relationships with others". This interpersonal – or social – intelligence "allows the individual to act and react properly with others. [...] It allows for empathy, cooperation, tolerance. [...] This form of intelligence can solve problems relating to relationships with others; [...] it is characteristic of leaders and organizers".

However, emotional intelligence was truly identified for the first time following the studies of Peter Salovey (born in 1958) and John D. Mayer (born in 1953) in the early 1990s. In their work, the two American psychologists defined emotional intelligence as "a form of intelligence that involves the ability to control one's own feelings and emotions, and those of others, to distinguish between them and to use this information to guide their thoughts and actions".

Inspired by their research, Daniel Goleman (PhD in clinical psychology and personal development) introduced the concept to the general public in his book *Emotional Intelligence* (1996). In this book, he defines emotional intelligence as "the ability [...] to identify, access and control one's own emotions and those of others in a group". This definition was completed the following year by Salovey and Mayer, who described EI as "the ability to perceive and express emotions, integrate to facilitate thought, understand and reason with emotion, as well as to regulate the emotions of oneself and of others". As for the term "emotional intelligence", this emerged in the late 1990s with the work of Reuven Bar-On (born in 1944), who was the first to measure this kind of intelligence. This writer focused his reflection on the concept of yield and success potential, focusing on different emotional and social skills: self-awareness, understanding and expression, awareness of others, managing strong emotions, good conflict resolution and adaptability. He defines emotional intelligence as follows: "Intelligence describes the aggregation of abilities, capabilities and skills [...]. The adjective 'emotional' is used to emphasise that this specific type of intelligence differs from cognitive intelligence". For Bar-On, emotional intelligence is likely to be improved through training and therapy.

The *Bar-On EQ-i*

Bar-On set up the first test of emotional quotient, the *Bar-On EQ-i*, in 1997. Participants responded to 133 statements ("In my daily life, my emotions often annoy me", "I can easily tell if someone is lying to me", "If I have a problem with somebody, I can easily talk to them", etc.) related to general life situations. Candidates had to answer using a scale from 1 to 5. After completing the questionnaire, the computer was able to calculate their emotional quotients based on five areas:

- intrapersonal skills;
- interpersonal skills;
- adaptability;
- stress management;
- overall mood.

Each point included five components such as assertiveness, stress tolerance, or impulse control.

Professional context

Later, Daniel Goleman developed the concept of emotional intelligence by exploring it in the workplace and educational environments. According to him, emotional intelligence "promotes professional and personal success". He adds that emotional intelligence allows children to be less aggressive and, later, to make the right decisions. In his book, *Emotional Intelligence at Work*, he puts forward the concept of "leadership resonance", which he defines as "the ability to put one's team on the same emotional wavelength and transmit one's own optimism and enthusiasm [...] as opposed to leadership of dissonance, which produces an emotionally toxic environment [...]".

EMOTIONAL INTELLIGENCE AND LEADERSHIP

What makes a good leader? To embody effective leadership, you need to motivate your team and raise positive emotions among employees. A good leader

For Goleman, good emotional intelligence in the workplace leads to high self-awareness and good self-management, but also a strong awareness of others and good management of social relationships. Establishing a direct link with neurology, the psychologist argues that the moods and actions of a team leader have an impact – whether positive or negative – on their employees. In other words, when a person sends signals, these may modify the hormone levels, heart rate and, in some cases, the immune system of another individual. This is what he calls "interpersonal limbic regulation".

Neuroscientist Elkhonon Goldberg (born in 1946) goes even further in his work from the early 2000s. He differentiates the right hemisphere, which is used to learn, to innovate and to explore, from the left hemisphere, which serves to store knowledge, memorise and analyse. Both hemispheres have different roles in managing emotions, namely, positive emotions are managed by the left hemisphere, and negative emotions are managed by the right hemisphere. Goldberg therefore concludes that if an individual is largely experiencing negative emotions, he will not have the ability to be creative or innovative, as the right hemisphere is already overstretched. Hence the importance of managing emotions, particularly on a professional level.

Significance of these theories

Although these theories have some variations, they agree on one major point: emotional intelligence can be developed, notably through training and coaching sessions.

Moreover, they particularly emphasise that not all achievements are attributed solely to IQ. Indeed, two people with the same IQ are unlikely to achieve equivalent educational and professional success, and this difference is clearly due to the emotional quotient. As early as 1944, psychologist David Wechsler (1896-1981) stated that "individuals with similar IQs could differ greatly in their ability to control their environment". Daniel Goleman therefore concluded that EQ is a better indicator of academic and professional success than IQ. However, the notion of IQ is very broad – we must consider economic intelligence, mathematical intelligence, etc. – therefore we can expect the concept of emotional intelligence to evolve, as there is much still left to discover.

EXTRA INFORMATION

Emotional intelligence is essential in certain professional fields, such as human resources management, team management, entrepreneurship, etc. Similarly, those with a high emotional quotient will find it easier

Different models

As the concept of emotional intelligence is relatively new, different EI models are competing with one another.

- **According to Salovey and Mayer, emotional intelligence is not only measurable by emotions but by knowledge** (which is based on learning and memory). Part of our EQ therefore comes from experience, which allows us to react and perceive emotions without understanding them. This dimension is considered a reflex.
- **According to Daniel Goleman, emotions interact with motivations** (directed by the needs of survival and reproduction). Psychologists make use of four concepts: self-awareness, self-control, social awareness and relationship management. It is this last model that we will look at more closely in the following section.
- **The model of Reuven Bar-On is based on the concept of emotional and social skills.** According to Bar-On, emotional intelligence combines skills, abilities and capabilities that can be developed through training and therapy. Reuven Bar-On identifies five components of emotional intelligence: intrapersonal skills, interpersonal skills, adaptability, stress management and overall mood.

IDENTIFYING EMOTIONAL SKILLS

The first step for those who wish to develop their EQ is to identify their emotional skills and learn to identify those of others. Then, they can really start to work on their feelings (trust, empathy, optimism, etc.) in order to improve their relationships with others. It is therefore essential, initially, to pinpoint the negative emotions that invade us regularly (anger, jealously, frustration, envy, anxiety, etc.), before using this knowledge to work on our skills.

To achieve this, we must be aware that an emotion is created in response to a change between the individual and the environment. Thus, anger can be a reaction to injustice or to an attack, while fear responds to danger, and so on. These emotions lead to different behaviours, such as avoidance, aggression, or withdrawing oneself. A high emotional quotient will thus allow you to be more sociable, better understand others, etc.: it is an ability that can lead to both a great career and a stable and fulfilling private life.

The list of emotional skills that we possess or that are within our reach is very long and varies according to each individual. However, some of them are fundamental to obtain a high emotional quotient. Each skill or emotion here is divided into four categories, according to the Goleman model: self-awareness, which allows for knowledge of oneself; self-management, which allows us to better manage any professional situation; awareness of others, which allows us to know others and their emotions; and finally, relationship management, which allows us to influence and understand the emotions of others.

Self-awareness

- **Self-confidence:** Confidence goes hand in hand with relaxation. Faced with a confident person, others feel reassured. Also, when someone has full confidence in themselves, they do not shy away from any difficulty, as nothing seems insurmountable.
- **Emotional awareness:** This involves identifying and understanding our own emotions. Emotional awareness facilitates the understanding of our strengths and weaknesses, and thus our own limitations. Intuitively, the individual will adopt the appropriate gesture for a better professional performance.
- **Self-assessment:** Good self-assessment helps us to take a step back to compare our strengths and weaknesses. The ability to put things into perspective will generally result in improvement in areas where we are weaker. This also makes it easier to accept criticism.
- **Self-regulation:** The ability to self-regulate means not giving in to impulses and maintaining inner balance. This concept also implies that we must learn to be relaxed and be better organised.
- **Intuition:** Intuition allows us to anticipate and avoid many conflicts, as well as to identify the appropriate time for discussion or action.

Self-management

- **Impulse control:** This ability facilitates the adaptation of behaviour in different situations.

- **Self-control:** Good self-control means we can maintain composure in any situation.
- **Self-esteem:** The image we have of ourselves naturally influences how others perceive us. It is therefore crucial to have good self-esteem.
- **Adaptability:** Great adaptability allows us to be effective in any situation and able to handle multiple tasks without losing sight of the original objectives.
- **Motivation:** A motivated person will be better able to take initiative, persevere and be effective.
- **Persistence:** A persistent individual will do anything to achieve their objectives, and is therefore more likely to achieve them.
- **Stress tolerance:** If the body is stressed, it sends stress signals to others, who are likely to become stressed themselves. In addition, stress makes us use up much more energy.
- **Optimism:** An optimistic person will have a positive impact on the motivation of the person they are dealing with and will not give up, even in the event of failure.
- **Flexibility:** Being flexible is a key skill for adapting to new challenges, as well as changes within a company.
- **Initiative:** An individual with good initiative can bring positive energy to others and be a motor for new ideas. This capability pushes them to seize– or even creates – new opportunities.

Awareness of others

- **Empathy:** Empathy helps us to tune into the people we are speaking to, to listen to them and read between the lines of what they are saying. An empathetic individual has a great capacity to listen to and to understand others.

> **EMPLOYEE TIP**
>
> When working regularly as part of a team, it is better to learn to anticipate crisis situations by detecting the mood of your colleagues, in order to avoid conflict. Therefore, be sure to be on good terms with the members of your team, but also to make the effort to get to know each of them, so that you can adapt to each situation, whether conflictual or not.

- **Assertiveness:** Assertiveness is the art of knowing how to criticise and accept criticism, knowing how to say no and to stay honest and true to oneself. An assertive person will find it easier to get a message across to someone, even if it is negative.
- **Open-mindedness:** Being open-minded means being friendly and having a positive attitude towards the ideas put forward by others.

Relationship management

- **Interpersonal skills:** Getting along with others, influencing them and communicating with them.
- **Troubleshooting:** Someone who has the ability to solve problems will encourage dialogue and negotiation. They will strive to promote the search for solutions and will be attentive to the needs of others.

- **Influence:** Influence proves to be of great assistance when it comes to delivering a persuasive speech to one's team.
- **Teamwork:** The ability to motivate teammates and work together on a common goal.

EMOTIONAL INTELLIGENCE IN BUSINESS

It has been said that a high emotional quotient is an undeniable asset in the workplace. It is through this that an employee can more easily find a place in their team and within the company, but also be more likely to receive a promotion.

In *Emotional Intelligence at Work*, Daniel Goleman noted that emotional intelligence would have an impact on the future job market as certain skills will become indispensable, such as "having the ability to bounce back, take initiative and adapt".

In 2012, American neurobiologist Jaak Panksepp (born in 1943) linked several emotions with the motivation to work.

According to him, when crossing a threshold, we move from a "motivational state" to a strong emotion, depending on the intensity of the stimulus. He defined four major emotions that directly influence our motivation to work. They act on "individual creativity and the desire to explore".

- **Desire** leads to joy, and therefore to creativity, the desire to discover and to move forward.
- **Distress** causes sadness, which involves a risk of losing social contact.
- **Anger** arouses aggression which, when channelled, can be useful for stopping or advancing a project.
- **Fear** triggers avoidance and leads to inactivity, passive behaviour and defiance.

TOP TIPS

- Learn to identify your strengths and weaknesses. If you know your strengths, you can easily rely on them. Similarly, if you know your weaknesses, you will more easily be able to determine your limits.
- Dare. The more you dare to take risks, the more you will trust yourself and be able to push your limits. It is by venturing into the unknown that we gain better results.
- Learn to recognise the warning signs you show when anger begins to overflow, an anxiety attack strikes or any other situation generates tensions. The sooner you detect the signs that trigger your stress, the more you can stay in control.
- Keep an open mind. The more open you are to others, the more you will be able to empathise.
- Prioritise conversation. Optimal communication will avoid many conflicts. When others feel listened to, they will be more inclined to negotiate over the conflicting situation.

EXTRA INFORMATION

Emotional intelligence also involves deciphering nonverbal communication. As much as we need to be able to decipher that of others, we must also be aware of our own body language. It will be easier to send messages through your body language, and you will also be more able to understand others and their emotions by

- Learn from the past. Accept your responsibilities and learn to recognise your mistakes. This will allow you to be more open and to know yourself better.

  > "I have learned from my past mistakes. Now, when there is a problem, I never react straight away. I know I have not handled my anger and irritation very well before, so I prefer to wait until these emotions have died down, so that I can discuss the issue calmly afterwards." – Rachel, administrative assistant for a non-profit organisation

- Be optimistic. It is easier to identify solutions and to see the best in others (and in ourselves) when we are optimistic.
- Be outgoing. The more outgoing you are, the more you will have the ability to influence others positively.
- Learn to recognise your value. List your skills, contacts and completed projects. Becoming aware of your value will boost your self-esteem.
- Relax. The calmer you are, the more others will be open for discussion. Being calm reduces stress and also lowers the risk of emotional overflow.

  > "Professionally, I have had many difficulties in the past, because I focused on family problems instead of my professional life. I was not in a good stage of my life and I also did not have a very high opinion of myself; I let myself be influenced by the criticism around me. Since then, I have changed, I feel better and now I have confidence in myself. I had several job offers and found a place which would have seemed unat-

tainable before. As they sense my self-confidence, people seem to also want to trust me." – Miya, employee in the hospitality sector

FAQS

When we are stressed, we send stress signals to those around us, who also become stressed in turn. We turn a trivial situation into a tense and uncomfortable situation. Stress also consumes a lot of energy, which weakens us during really tough times. It also prevents us from controlling our emotions: a tense situation then leads more quickly to an overflow of emotions and increases the risk of conflict.

TECHNIQUES FOR RELAXATION AT WORK

There are several relaxation techniques that you can practice at your place of work to better manage stress.

- If you feel stress beginning to build, take a walk, away from your desk and take a break.
- A simple gesture that we often forget to do at work: drink water. Stress and dehydration are closely related!
- Focus on your breathing to help eliminate tension. Inhale deeply and exhale slowly through the abdomen. Your heart rate will immediately slow down and your nervous system will gradually calm down.
- Stretch. Stretch your legs and your arms, and circle your head a few times.
- Monitor how tired your eyes are. Eyes are not

designed to stay in front of a computer screen for several hours, so it is important to rest them as much as possible. To do this, there are two techniques: close your eyes and place your hands on your closed eyelids. The darkness and heat will allow them to recharge quickly. The second technique is to draw an infinity sign repeatedly with your eyes.

WHY IS EMPATHY AN ESSENTIAL ELEMENT IN THE DEVELOPMENT OF EMOTIONAL QUOTIENT?

Empathy allows you to be attentive to others, to better understand them and to better anticipate their reactions. Being empathetic also develops openness and assertiveness. The more empathetic you are, the less you are centred on yourself, which allows you to communicate better with others.

WHAT SKILLS WILL ENABLE ME TO GROW WITHIN MY COMPANY?

In his research, Daniel Goleman identifies four critical skills for professional success: self-confidence, the ability to adapt and to bounce back, initiative and the ability to cooperate with others. These skills are essential for progress in today's employment market. Jaak Panksepp, the neurobiologist, states that it is primarily desire that drives the creativity and motivation required in the professional world.

HOW CAN I PUT A STRONG EMOTION, SUCH AS ANGER, TO GOOD USE?

A powerful emotion drains a lot of potential for action. When acting out of a strong emotion, we must be aware of it and control it. Thus, anger can be devastating at work; yet, if it is properly channelled, it can turn into productive aggressiveness. With this aggressiveness, it is sometimes easier to support a project or to begin a difficult task.

HOW CAN I GIVE CONSTRUCTIVE CRITICISM TO A CO-WORKER?

The best way to give constructive criticism is to adopt assertive and empathetic behaviour: consider the emotions of the person in front of you, as well as your own. By putting yourself in another's shoes, it is easier to have an honest talk and to better understand their message.

Specifically, a good trick for criticising without attacking is to formulate your sentences beginning with "I", not "you". "I would like to have your attention", rather than "You're not listening", for example. You can express your views without appearing to judge another. This formulation also helps to keep the dialogue open: they have the opportunity to respond to your feelings and express their own views. They will not feel challenged, while understanding that they can do better.

HOW CAN I USE MY EMOTIONS AS A SOURCE OF SELF-MOTIVATION?

Four main emotions have an influence, whether positive or negative, on motivation, and therefore on action: desire, distress, anger and fear. To self-motivate facing a daunting task, which will create these emotions, you should try to feel in control so as to allow yourself to move forward.

It is usually desire, a positive feeling, which is most likely to provide the necessary energy to complete an uninspiring task. Try to find it in something that can generate desire: the desire to do well, the desire to meet a challenge, the desire to put something behind you, etc.

Distress, anger and fear can also prove effective incentives in certain situations. If, for example, injustice bothers you, but you have never taken action to change things, despite your desire to do so, you can try to focus on the anger caused by this situation to push you to take action; you can exploit your fear to embark on another project that frightens you less, but is still a challenge; you can turn your distress into a way of bringing the people around you together to achieve a common goal, etc.

What's important is to be aware of your emotions and able to use them wisely.

OVER TO YOU

GET TO KNOW YOURSELF BETTER

- Start by asking yourself the right questions. At the end of the day, analyse your actions: "Why did I act in that way?", "What in this meeting caused conflict?", "Did I misspeak?", "Was my attitude narrow-minded?", "Did I unwittingly send negative signals?", etc.
- Evaluate yourself at the end of each week, list your strengths and weaknesses from the week in a notebook to allow you to step back and see your limits, motivations and shortcomings. Periodically review your notes as this will help you to see any potential improvement and inspire self-confidence.

LEARNING MORE ABOUT OTHERS

- Test your interpretation of others by watching the television on mute and trying to guess what everyone is saying through their body language and attitude.
- Keep a memory book on your professional circle. Each night, ask yourself how your colleagues were dressed, whether they were smiling, what they said to you, etc. This will allow you to be a better observer and have better knowledge of others.
- Force yourself to talk to others. Do you know the receptionist well? Go and see them for five minutes each day, ask them how they are doing, and try to learn more about them.
- Choose a loved one who is experiencing a difficult situa-

tion and imagine yourself in their place. How would you have reacted if you were in the same situation? Why did they react in that way? How did they feel?

CONTROL YOUR EMOTIONS

- Boost your confidence by taking the time to dress yourself well. A few classy wardrobe items that are suitable for your job will help your self-esteem.
- Practice relaxation. By being more serene, you will develop better nonverbal communication. You will not send stress signals to others. If relaxation or yoga is not for you, exercise instead.

BENSON EXERCISE

This technique, introduced by Herbert Benson, a professor at Harvard University is for relaxing in ten minutes. Choose a word that has positive connotations for you (lovely, love, sun, etc.); then select an image that speaks to you (a beach, fields, etc.); now, close your eyes, relax as you breathe through the abdomen and say your chosen word in your head while exhaling, while picturing the image you selected.

- To improve your optimism, start by appreciating your skills and those of others. Learn to see the good side of things, even the most difficult situations. Learn to laugh at your mistakes.
- Work on your negative emotions and learn to anticipate

them.

Scenario

Anticipate conflicts by picturing yourself in a difficult imaginary situation. Imagine your reactions and those of others. In doing so, you are training your mind to have better reactions in the event of conflict or unexpected problems.

Similarly, when you have an important presentation or interview, imagine the scene and put yourself in the situation. During your imaginary presentation, imagine experiencing success. This will condition your mind to be confident and optimistic on the day.

- During a confrontational exchange, do not let your emotions do the talking. Delay by asking your partner to rephrase, listen carefully and try to understand what they expect from you. This will allow you to silence your emotions and let reason speak.

The issue of formulation

Learn to adopt an assertive manner. Similarly, it is better to avoid temporal adverbs, such as "never" or "always". Also, use "I" instead of "you", to refrain from attacking the person you are talking to.

We want to hear from you!
Leave a comment on your online library
and share your favourite books on social media!

FURTHER READING

BIBLIOGRAPHY

- Demarquet, F. (No date) L'intelligence émotionnelle. *FredericdeMarquet.com.* [Online]. [Accessed 20 May 2015]. Available from: <http://www.fredericdemarquet.com/sites/default/files/support_lintelligence_emotion-nelle.pdf>
- Direction-Performance. (No date) *Qu'est-ce que l'intelligence émotionnelle au travail.* [Online]. [Accessed 20 May 2015]. Available from: <http://direction-performance.be/cest-quoi/quest-ce-que- lintelligence-emotionnelle-au-travail/>
- Fauconnier, F. (2007) Le quotient émotionnel: passeport pour la réussite. Journal du net. [Online]. [Accessed 5 May 2015]. Available from: <http://www.journaldunet.com/management/0706/quotient-emotionnel/>
- Gardner, H. (1983) *Frames of Mind: the Theory of Multiple Intelligence.* New York: Basic Books.
- Goleman, D. (1996) *Emotional Intelligence.* New York: Bantam Books.
- Goleman, D. (1998) *Emotional Intelligence at Work*, New York, Bantam Books.
- Guéret, C. (No date) Cultivez votre intelligence émotionnelle. *Psychologies.com.* [Online]. [Accessed 5 May 2015]. Available from: <http://www.psychologies.com/Moi/Se-connaitre/Personnalite/Articles-et-Dossiers/Comment-developper-votre-intuition/Cultivez-votre-intelligence-emotionnelle>
- Mayer, J. D., Forgas, J. P., and Ciarrochi , J. (1997)

Emotional Intelligence in Everyday Life: A Scientific Inquiry. New York: Taylor & Francis.
- Panksepp, J. and Biven, L. (2012) *The Archaeology of Mind: Neuroevolutionary Origins of Human Emotions*. New York: W.W. Norton & Company.
- Rhee, K. and White, R. (2007) *Journal of Small Business and Entrepreneurship*. 20(4). [Online]. [Accessed 20 May 2015]. Available from: <http://www.freepatentsonline.com/article/Journal-SmallBusiness-Entrepreneurship/204986722.html>
- Roussel, D. (No date) Gestion du stress: Gérer et prévenir le stress au travail. *IRCAR Formation*. [Online]. [Accessed 10th May 2015]. Available from: <http://www.ircar-formation.com/medias/files/les-gestes-simples-pour-recuperer-en-5-minutes-1.pdf>

www.50minutes.com

Ebook EAN: 9782806279255

Paperback EAN: 9782806284204

Legal Deposit: D/2016/12603/366

Cover: © Primento

Digital conception by Primento, the digital partner of publishers.

Made in the USA
Monee, IL
07 July 2026